THE CHEETAH

Fast as Lightning

Text and photos by

Christine and Michel Denis-Huot

French series editor, Valérie Tracqui

i≙i Charlesbridge

© 2002 by Editions Milan under the title *Le Guépard*
300 rue Léon-Joulin, 31101 Toulouse Cedex 100, France
French series editor, Valérie Tracqui

Published by Charlesbridge
85 Main Street
Watertown, MA 02472
(617) 926-0329
www.charlesbridge.com

Library of Congress Cataloging-in-Publication Data
Denis-Huot, Christine.
   [Guépard. English]
   The cheetah / Christine and Michel Denis-Huot ; [translated
by Randi Rivers].
      p. cm. — (Animal close-ups)
Summary: Describes the habits, characteristics, and habitat of
cheetahs. Includes bibliographical references.
   ISBN-13: 978-1-57091-626-7 (softcover)
   ISBN-10: 1-57091-626-8 (softcover)
   1. Cheetahs—Juvenile literature. [1. Cheetah.] I. Denis-Huot,
Michel. II. Title. III. Series.
   QL737.C23D44 2004
   599.75'9—dc21   2003006332

Printed in China
(sc) 10 9 8 7 6 5 4 3

PHOTO CREDITS
All photos are by Christine and Michel Denis-Huot except the following:
L. C. Marigo/P. Arnol/Bios: 27 (top); Klein/Hubert/Bios: 27 (middle)

KEEPING WATCH

In Africa on the plains of Kenya, the bush fires of the dry season have been extinguished by the downpours of the rainy season. The savanna is covered with green grass, drawing herds of animals to graze. Gazelles gather to eat in the heat of the afternoon. Impalas rest in the shade of small acacias. All is peaceful. Until . . .

A cheetah hidden in the tall grass wakes from its nap. It climbs a large termite mound and surveys its surroundings. The cheetah is hungry and the gazelles would make an excellent meal.

The cheetah takes its time in choosing prey. It waits to attack until a gazelle strays from the herd. Creeping closer to the young gazelle, the cheetah keeps a steady eye on its prey. The cheetah is ready to pounce when suddenly the herd senses danger. The herd scatters and the cheetah returns to its hiding spot, waiting for another chance.

Cheetahs live on savannas and semi-desert ranges. They hide in tall grass and bushes to secretly watch prey or to escape from predators.

Cheetahs use high places, such as termite mounds, to keep a close eye on grazing herds and potential predators.

Cheetahs' fur is gold to dark ocher, marked with black spots, or rosettes, which allow them to stalk through tall yellow grass unnoticed.

CHAMPION RUNNERS

Cheetahs are lightweight; females weigh around 88 pounds, and males can weigh up to 140 pounds. Their large nostrils and lungs allow for quick intake of air while running.

Thanks to their excellent vision, cheetahs can see their prey clearly from a great distance. Since they are daytime hunters, cheetahs rely on their eyesight to spot prey.

Unlike other felines, cheetahs' claws are not retractable. Their claws act as cleats, allowing cheetahs to keep a good grip on the ground at all times. Even at full speed cheetahs can turn abruptly, with their 30-inch tail helping them balance. Running 70 miles per hour at top speed, cheetahs are the fastest animals on earth. They use so much energy running, however, that they can't run for long periods of time.

Cheetahs have sleek, athletic bodies designed for running.

Very Flexible

A cheetah's spine is flexible, acting much like a spring. When preparing to sprint, a cheetah arches its back to tighten the spine and crosses its front and back paws. Then it loosens its spine, launching into a sprint. Cheetahs can reach speeds of 45 miles per hour in two seconds.

Cheetahs have black "tearstains" that run from their eyes to their lips. It's believed this cuts down on sun glare, letting cheetahs keep a steady eye on their prey.

A cheetah's spots form different patterns on each animal. Black bands ring its tail, which is tipped with white fur.

7

THE CHASE

Cheetahs hunt early in the morning or at dusk when it is not as hot. Cheetahs spot their prey from high places. If they can, cheetahs choose injured or old animals to make their hunt easier. The cheetah advances stealthily, neck tensed, with a steady gaze on its prey. Many times a cheetah spots a young gazelle wandering away from the herd. If the herd senses danger, it will become uneasy and the hunt will be ruined. Cheetahs have infinite patience and keep still until the herd calms down and continues to eat.

Cheetahs strike quickly and by surprise. If an attack fails, a cheetah must rest for a half-hour to regain its speed. Running at such high speeds takes a lot of energy.

Sometimes a clever cheetah chases a baby gazelle since it knows the animal cannot run fast.

Cheetahs use speed to their advantage. They unbalance and knock over their prey so it falls onto its back, defenseless.

After cheetahs immobilize their prey, they kill it.

Once cheetahs are sure they are undetected, they can sneak within 300 feet without alerting their prey. By the time an animal sees a cheetah, it's too late. An animal may run in a zigzag in an attempt to escape, but once a cheetah knocks over its prey with its paw, the fight is over.

QUICK MEAL

Hunting exhausts cheetahs. They rest for 20 minutes to regain their strength before eating. As they rest, cheetahs carefully survey their surroundings to avoid surprise attacks by predators. Vultures fly overhead and try to steal their prey. Cheetahs remain on guard while they eat.

Cheetahs eat antelope such as gazelles and impalas. When they can't find antelope, cheetahs resort to smaller prey such as hares or guinea fowl.

Cheetahs try to ward off vultures that attempt to steal their prey, but they will quickly abandon the meal if the vultures become too persistent.

Males split a gazelle that they killed together. Several cheetahs working together can attack an adult wildebeest.

If disturbed while eating, cheetahs will leave their prey and never return. Unlike lions, cheetahs will only eat what they themselves have killed. Adults need six pounds of meat per day on average, but they can eat 30 pounds in a single meal and this will nourish them for several days.

Attention Thieves

Too often cheetahs must leave their meal to bigger predators, including lions, hyenas, panthers, and even male baboons. Cheetahs aren't armed to defend their prey, and they don't carry their prey into trees like panthers do. If a cheetah tries to save its meal, it could lose its life.

Cheetahs kill their prey by suffocating it. They bite an animal's throat, blocking its windpipe.

THEY MEET

Adult females live alone unless they are raising cubs. Within their territory, females live solitary lives, following the gazelles that migrate from season to season.

Cheetahs mate year-round. When she is ready to mate, a female cheetah will enter territory occupied by males. To let them know she's ready to mate, she urinates in the bushes at the edge of their territory. The males are excited and search for the female. They yelp to attract her attention.

The female rolls in the grass when they find her. She's ready to mate. Only the dominant male cheetah of the group mates with the female cheetah. The males and female stay together for three days. Then the female returns to her territory while the males remain on theirs.

Males patrol their territory and mark it with urine.

Males can live alone, like females, but they prefer to associate with 2 or 3 other males, usually siblings, to acquire a territory. Their union lasts a lifetime.

Males fight intruders who may try to take their territory.

BABIES ARRIVE!

After three months of pregnancy, females give birth to their cubs in a den surrounded by tall grass. Cubs have dark stomachs and light backs. They are born with their eyes shut and are completely helpless. Mothers move their cubs every few days to evade predators. They do this until the cubs are able to walk on their own.

A mother will move her cubs one at a time, carrying them in her mouth to a new hiding spot.

Females can give birth to 8 babies, but the average is between 2 and 5. The weakest cubs die at birth.

Females raise their cubs alone. It's risky leaving cubs unattended to go hunting, because lions, hyenas, or panthers could kill them. Buffaloes traveling near the den could trample the cubs. The cubs' chances of survival are slim. One out of three cubs dies before it reaches the age of three months.

Mothers only leave their cubs to hunt, then quickly return. Cheetah cubs make chirping sounds, like birds, letting their mother know when it's time to nurse. After they've nursed, their mother massages the cubs' stomachs by licking them with her tongue. This helps the cubs digest their food.

Cubs are small at birth and must drink a lot of milk to gain weight.

Cheetah cubs purr as they knead their mother's teat to get milk.

GROWING UP

At the end of several days, cheetah cubs take their first steps. They grow fast. At five weeks they are able to follow their mother on short trips. If a cub wanders too far from its mother, she will call it back to her. It's a dangerous time. On the plains predators can see the cubs, but the cubs aren't fast enough to escape.

When it's time to hunt, mothers call for their cubs to hide. Cubs are sometimes disobedient and can follow their mother on the hunt. Of course, the gazelles see the cubs, and the hunt is ruined. Mothers let out a growl to make their cubs obey. Then they quickly run off to hunt. Bringing back small prey, mothers share the meat with their cubs. If there is not enough to feed them all, mothers will go back out on the hunt.

Like their mother, cubs learn to watch over their territory.

After their meal, cheetahs find some shade. The cubs are playful and wrestle with their mother. She knocks them over with a tap of her paw and licks them. Full of tenderness, mother cheetahs enjoy playing with their cubs.

Cubs are too vulnerable to be left alone on the savanna.

At the end of several weeks, cheetah cubs begin to turn the same color as their mother. Their silvery mane disappears at about 3 months.

Cubs nurse until they are 3 months old. Nursing takes its toll on mothers, making them very tired. Mothers need to eat a lot to produce enough milk for their cubs.

17

ON GUARD

At two months cheetah cubs can accompany their mother everywhere. When the mother hunts, her cubs stay in hiding, waiting for a signal to join in the meal. Feeding a litter of cheetahs is difficult. She must hunt every day, whereas a solitary female can satisfy herself with prey every two or three days.

Large predators, such as lions, pose a great threat to cheetah cubs. Mothers cry out in alarm to their cubs, but sometimes it's too late. Lions attack by surprise before a cub can run away.

Cubs always eat first. When prey is small, mothers have nothing to eat and must hunt some more to feed themselves.

Washing each other after meals helps keep fur clean.

Cubs learn how to attack and how to recover from an ambush.

Cubs exercise their back, neck, and paws by leaping around and tussling with each other. Play helps the cubs develop quick reflexes.

Lions kill by shaking cheetah cubs and throwing them to the ground. In most cases lions kill the cubs but don't eat them. No one knows why they do this, but it may be because lions and cheetahs compete for the same prey. The surviving cubs carry on with their daily routine. They play, each taking a turn at being the predator or the prey.

HUNTING SCHOOL

As weeks pass, the cubs observe their mother more often when she hunts. They learn the habits of their prey.

A mother cheetah may test her cubs' hunting skills by bringing back a small, live gazelle and releasing it under their noses. They don't know what to do. When the prey leaps up and runs away, cubs either try to follow without success or act disinterested. The mother observes the scene without interfering. If her cubs are unsuccessful, she will kill the antelope.

Time passes and the cubs' hunting techniques improve. They now know how to catch small prey and throw it to the ground, but they are still unsure how to kill it. Cubs learn to strangle their victims at around 10 months old.

At first cubs are confused about what they should do with the live prey their mother has brought. Their confusion gives the prey time to escape.

With more experience cubs succeed in capturing a young gazelle by themselves.

A cub's claws are still sharp, so it is able to climb trees. Adult cheetahs cannot do the same because their claws are dull from too much use.

Cubs claw tree trunks. When they are older, this will be a way they mark their territory.

SEPARATION

When cheetahs reach 18 months, their mother leaves. This time she does not return; she's gone off to find a mate. The young cheetahs have learned enough from their mother to survive on their own. They hunt together and divide their prey.

After another four months, a young female is old enough to have cubs. She leaves her brothers and sets off for a territory in or near where her mother currently lives. She will live alone until she has a litter of her own.

Young males live like nomads until they have the strength to conquer their own territory. Male cheetah siblings usually form a lasting union. They are affectionate and will rule their territory together.

If they can avoid predators and hunters, cheetahs can live about seven to 12 years.

Male cheetahs live together in groups and often show affection toward each other.

Mothers play with their cubs until the cubs are grown. Once daughters reach maturity, their mothers ignore them.

Young cheetahs catch small prey at first. The more they hunt, the more their skills improve.

FELINES IN DANGER

Cheetahs are in danger of becoming extinct. There are fewer each year. In national parks where they are protected, cheetahs are still in danger from larger predators, such as lions, and are sometimes threatened by tourists.

LOVED AND HUNTED

In 1900, there were 100,000 cheetahs worldwide. Now there are fewer than 10,000 in Africa. They have almost disappeared in Asia, except from Iran where there are fewer than 200. About a tenth of the cheetah population lives in captivity. Cheetahs have been tracked for their pelts for many years. Today cheetahs are classified as a protected species, but this doesn't deter South African farmers from killing them when cheetahs attack their livestock.

Due to the value of their fur, cheetahs have been hunted almost to the point of extinction.

These young cheetahs were raised in captivity, then released onto the reserve once they reached adulthood. They've gotten into the habit of climbing on tourist vehicles to play or watch over prey.

CONSERVATION EFFORTS

Farmers kill large numbers of cheetahs to protect their livestock. Educational programs aimed at teaching farmers ways of reducing cheetah threats to livestock have been put in place. Electric fences are one method of keeping cheetahs away from farm animals. This allows farmers and cheetahs to coexist in peace.

Scientists put collars with transmitters on cheetahs so they can follow the animals' daily movements and determine their needs.

REFUGE IN THE PARKS

In East Africa many cheetahs find refuge in national parks. But they cannot compete with hyenas and lions, whose numbers are on the rise. Big predators can steal a cheetah's prey and kill its young. In addition, cheetahs are disturbed in protected zones by tourists who scare away prey and ruin the hunt.

Born in the Zoo

Sylvie, a Doué-la-Fontaine Zoo nurse, works with cheetah cubs each day. These cubs are seen here at five weeks old. Cheetah births in captivity are rare.

CHEETAH COUSINS

Cheetahs are part of the large feline family, which is composed of 35 species. These carnivores are excellent hunters, stealthy and agile.

JAGUARS

Jaguars resemble leopards but are heavier and have larger paws and a huge head. Their spots resemble ring-like markings. Jaguars live in Central and South America where they are the biggest predators. They roam through thick bushes in the jungle, usually near water. Jaguars are good at fishing. These felines are threatened as their habitat is reduced day by day by humans.

SERVALS

Adult servals weigh between 13 and 33 pounds. They are much smaller than cheetahs. Like cheetahs, servals live on the African savanna. They are solitary animals and hunt in the tall grass, particularly for birds. They capture their prey by leaping on it and crushing it under their weight. A serval's dark spots are long on its back and round on its sides.

OCELOTS

Ocelots are the smallest of the spotted felines. Ocelots live in the forests of South and Central America. Ocelots are good swimmers and excellent climbers. They spend much of their time up in the trees, but they hunt on the ground for all sorts of prey. Ocelots were once hunted for their fur, but now they are protected.

SNOW LEOPARDS

Snow leopards are the rarest of the spotted felines. They live in the Himalayas in Asia. Their thick coats protect them from freezing temperatures, and their large paws keep them from sinking in the snow. Snow leopards make extraordinary leaps: as high as 20 feet and as long as 50 feet. In the past many were killed for their fur, and now there are only an estimated 3,500 to 7,000 left in the wild.

LEOPARDS

Leopards are much larger than cheetahs. Leopards live in Asia and Africa, climb trees well, and like to sleep there. They also bring their prey into the trees with them to avoid other predators who may try to steal it. Leopards hunt all night. Their spots are not always closed as the cheetah's appear to be.

For Further Reading on Cheetahs . . .

Grimbly, Shona. *Cheetahs* (*Endangered!* series). Tarrytown, NY: Marshall Cavendish Corporation, 1999.

Schlaepfer, Gloria G. *Cheetahs* (*Animal Ways* series). Tarrytown, NY: Benchmark Books, 2002.

Smyth, Alia. *Cheetahs* (*Nature's Children* series). Danbury, CT: Grolier Educational Corporation, 1989.

Use the Internet to Find Out More about Cheetahs . . .

The Cheetah Spot
—Learn interesting facts about cheetahs—from their appearance, to how they hunt, to how fast they can run. Also offers downloads of cheetah sounds.
http://www.cheetahspot.com

Cheetah.org
—The Cheetah Conservation Fund site features fun facts, pictures to color, and a cool movie to watch. Check out the article on how cheetahs got their spots.
http://www.cheetah.org

National Geographic Creature Feature: Cheetahs
—This site from National Geographic spotlights cheetahs and offers games and activities for kids. Kids can even send an electronic cheetah postcard to their friends.
http://www.nationalgeographic.com/kids/creature_feature/0003/cheetah.html

Index